THE BODY OF CANCER

(7 Strong Women)

DEBORAH SHIRLEY PEGUES

To order additional copies of this book, contact:
Xlibris
844-714-8691
www.Xlibris.com
Orders@Xlibris.com

ISBN: Softcover   979-8-3694-0722-6
           Harcover   979-8-3694-1749-2
           EBook   979-8-3694-0721-9

Library of Congress Control Number: 2023922278

Print information available on the last page

Rev. date: 03/04/2024

CHAPTER

The Checklist

"Hey mama. How you doing?"

No response.

"Mama." For some reason, Mama didn't respond to either of Effie's calling. As she walked through the house, she found her in the kitchen washing dishes. She attempted to call out to her again, but this time she walked over to her and touched her shoulder.

"Mammmmma!," Effie yelled. Startling her, Mama screamed, "Ahhhhhh!! – What is wrong with you girl? Don't be sneaking up on me like that. I'm not chicken, but you almost caught a two-piece" (showing her right & left fist).

"Mama, I didn't sneak up on you. I called your name several times."

"I had my noise cancelling air pods in my ears listening to my gospel music," doing a traditional Baptist Sunday Morning Choir rock.

She was already taken a back with the thought of her Mama keeping up with the times with an I-phone, but she was shocked that she even knew what an air pod was. Headphones, yes – air pods, not so much.

"Who bought you air pods?" Effie asked in a unapproving tone.

Mama replied, "And just who are you questioning? If you must know, I bought them myself. You make it seem like I am too old to have air pods. It is 2023 you know."

Although it seemed weird, Effie couldn't debate it. "Well…. I think it is dangerous. What if there was an emergency and you didn't hear what was going on?

"Effie, what's the problem? Unresponsive to her question, Mama continued – "Girl, you are always worrying about stuff that ain't happened yet. Focus on what's going on now, like you passing me that plate."

Laughing and shaking her head at the same time, Effie asked, "How are you mama? Everything good?"

"I'm good. I mean, there's always something going on, but life don't stop because something's going on. I just keep it pushing. I can't move forward if I am constantly looking back."

"Yes, Mama I understand." Mumbling under her breath, but loud enough for Mama to hear.

"You understand?" Knowing her daughter better than her daughter knows herself, Mama says,

"Alright let me hear it."

"Hear what?," she replied as if her Mama didn't know her better than she knows herself. *"You know what I'm talking about. You didn't just stop by here for nothing."* Doing what Mama's do, she simply stared at Effie waiting for her to begin.

"How do you always know?" Just as soon as she asked this question, both Mama and Effie said in unison, *"It's a mother's job to know."*

"Ok, so now tell me what's going on -or shall I go down my checklist?

"Your checklist? What checklist?"

When asked to explain, Mama dried her hands from the soap water and prepared herself to hip Effie to what every mother has in their possession – The Checklist.

"A Mother's Checklist – A Checklist of what is going on with your children,

when you know something is going on with your children, but your children like to beat around the bush instead of preserving the time they are wasting by not saying what they want checklist."

"Ohhhhh, that checklist."

Feeling good, Mama asked, *"Now, shall I proceed?"* Answering her own question Mama replies,

"Yes indeed." You need money?"

"Well….," cutting her off, *"Don't have none. Next, you pregnant?"*

Effie embarrassingly shouts, *"Mama no!"*

Laughing at her own checklist, Mama says, *"Ok. Well, that's the end of my checklist. What's up?"*

"Mama, I just need to talk to you; more importantly, I need you to listen."

Hearing the seriousness in her tone, she gives her full attention. *"Okay. I'm listening Effie, waiting for you to talk."*

"Mama, I - I don't really know how to say this." Now deeply concerned. *"What is it Effie?" "Well mama, I......."*

"Mama, Mama, guess what?" Running in the house is Lyna, Mama's other daughter and Effie's younger sister.

"Now Lyna, you know better than to come into this house yelling at the top of your lungs like you do when you're singing off key in the church choir."

Touching her throat and placing one finger in her right ear, Lynn belts out, **"Woooooo – Woo Woo Woo!! Now Mama you know I got vocals. Hey Effie."**

"Hey girl," *Effie said while laughing and shaking her head at her sister.*

"Did I interrupt something?" *Lyna asked.* **"YES, I was getting ready to talk to Effie about something that I believe is very important." "No"** *(Effie)*

Sensing something is going on Lyna whispers, **"Was y'all praying or something?"**

"Lyna how many times do I have to tell you that you never enter anywhere loudly because you don't know what's going on in there before you enter."

Counting in her head the number of times she has been told this. **"You tell me that all the time mama, but the bible says enter His gates with thanksgiving and into His courts with praise. So.....who should I listen to mama?**

Looking for something to throw, Mama replies, **"Girl, don't play with me. Your sister and I are having a conversation."**

"Uggggh - About what?"

"Well, I don't know. Something or shall I say someone flew in from the cuckoo's nest before I could find out." *Not resisting the urge to be sarcastic, Lyna jumps at the opportunity.* **"What... Mama you didn't tell me you had a bird. Where is it?"** *Effie couldn't help but laugh at Lyna's sarcastic yet comedic timing.*

"Girrrrrrl, what is wrong with you" *replied Effie.*

"Just hush Lyna. Now Effie, go on and tell me what's wrong." *Feeling that the timing was no longer right, along with the fact that she couldn't talk around nosey Lyna, Effie changed the subject.* **"Never mind Mama. I'll be back – I'm going to the store. Do you need anything? We can talk when I get back."**

"Yes, baby can you bring me back some uhh.. wait, let me grab my checklist." *Shaking her head, Effie responds,* **"You love your checklists don't you?"** *Seconding that response, Lyna confirms.* **"Girl you know about the checklist too. I never get past number 1. Hold up Effie, I am going to ride with you. Bye Mama."**

"Now where are you going Lyna. You came rushing in here, interrupting us saying, "mama, mama, guess what?" So, what is it? What did you need to tell me? *Running out the door, Lyna yells,* **"I'll tell you later mama. I'm going with Effie. Bye."**

Not understanding what just happened, Mama has a conversation with God (and herself) to gain some clarity.

"Lord, help me. I don't know what's going on with my daughters, but I got housework to do. One come by and don't know what she's trying to say and the other one come in and turn everything around. Somebody better start telling me something soon. I'm getting ready to put back on my air pods. If this don't ……"

Mama stops mid-sentence as she hears her front door open. **"Now who's coming in the door?"** *Mama pauses for a moment and then said,* **"OMG it's my other two daughters Ashley and Mercedes, along with their friends Fatima and Taraji.**

"Now what do they want?"

CHAPTER

The Reveal

"Heyyyyyyyyyyyyyyyy Mama," said Ashley in a cartoonish voice.

"Now haven't I told you that hey is for horses Ashley!!" *"My bad."* Correcting herself, Ashley gives a revised yet proper England greeting. *"Hello Mother."*

"Good morning ma. How are you?" asked Mercedes. *"I'm good Mercedes. Good morning Fatima / Taraji. Uhhh where y'all coming from?"*

Well, we were on our way to the mall, but...I needed to talk with you for a second," replied Mercedes.

I need to talk to you too Mama, and I wanted to talk first,"

Well, you won't be 1ˢᵗ. I was already talking to Effie, and then Lyna interrupted her. They went to the store and now I'm waiting on them to come back. I believe you are after Lyna Mercedes, and then I'll talk to you 4ᵗʰ Ashley. Is that ok? Something is going on and I know its not Mother's Day cuz we in the month of February. All my daughters have wanted my attention today. When those other two get back, we are going to get to the bottom of this.

Now before they get back, do I need to go down my checklist with you two?"

In unison, both Ashley and Taraji sing, *"Noooooooooooooo!!"*

"Well, we're all family so why can't we all say what we need to say? Unless it's a deep dark secret. Is it a deep dark secret?"

With one looking down, while the other looked out into space - they remained silent.

"Now when I ask a question, everybody suddenly want to get quiet. Like you're under arrest or something. Believe me what you say can and will be used against you in the house of Precious."

"So, Ashley you can go ahead and talk. I will talk to you later mom," replied Mercedes.

At a loss for words, Ashley said, *"Ummm... Effie was first. I can also wait Mama. Mercedes did come in before me."*

Returning from the store, Effie and Lyna enter the house noticing their sisters and friends are there.

"Heyyyyyyyy ya'll," yelled Lyna. Effie began unloading the grocery bags. *"Here is everything that was on your list mom. They just didn't have the cinnamon and nutmeg. They were all out."* Mama just sat quietly.

Effie continued, *"**Mama, is that ok? I can try another store.**" "**No Effie. I just won't be coking yams for tomorrow's dinner.**" Lyna looking puzzled. "**Is it a special dinner? What's going on?**"*

Mama, sarcastically replied, *"**Well I found out that mother's day has been moved to February because all my beautiful daughters need one on one time with me. Now before anyone leaves to go to any malls or anywhere else, I need to know what is going on with all you all. Each one of you said you need to tell me something - yet no one wants to talk in front of the family. We are a family. Whatever it is, it will be alright. Especially since all you all have passed my checklist. Now Effie, you're the oldest. Talk to me.**"*

Visibly upset, Fatima responded, *"**No Mama please.**"*

*"**No Effie, I need you to talk. Even your friends spoke up and said it's time. I want to know what they are talking about.**"*

Taraji interjected saying, *"**Respectfully, Mama Precious, its time for all of them to talk.**"*

All this delay in speaking what is wrong is growing tired and now Mama's frustrated. *"**TALK !! - I'm the one who needs to be reclaiming my time. Y'all are only standing here wasting it.**"*

Immediately, everyone starts talking at once over each other. " *"**Now how am I supposed to hear all of you at one time.**"* By this point, Effie had reached her boiling point and interrupts all of them.

*"**Enough!! Enough!! I'm tired and I can't keep it anymore. I have Cancer.**"*

The room fell quiet as everyone's eyes and heart turned to Effie. *"**Did you hear me Mama? I have breast cancer.**"*

*"**Effie baby,**"* said Mama as tears filled her eyes. *"**Oh no not my baby.**"* As Mama held Effie in her arms crying, Lyna raised her hung down head and said, *"**Me too Mama.**"*

Mama and Effie released each other and turned their attention to Lyna. *"**I have stomach cancer.**** Falling to her knees and holding Mama's waist. "**Oh Mama.**"*

*"**I tried to tell you in the kitchen, but you kept bringing out your checklist.**"* As she slowly stands to her feet, Lyna continued. *"**I don't want anyone feeling sorry for me. I didn't want to put my problems and stress on no one else. Mama, do you understand why I couldn't say anything?**"*

*"**I do understand, but what I need for you all to understand is when you cry, I cry; when you laugh, I laugh. We are in this together.**"*

With so much being revealed, Mercedes needed a moment to herself. *"I just can't believe all of this. I need to leave. I can't take this right now."* As she prepared to leave, Fatima stopped her. *"Mercedes, No! Talk to your family now."* Taraji followed saying, *"You too Ashley."*

"Will you please tell me what is going on?," pleaded Mama. *"Mercedes tell me."*

(Mercedes) "Pelvic Cancer." (Ashley) "Bone Cancer."

Mama stood there in utter disbelief. *"My God, My God. Ohhhhhh Lord today. I hear you Lord. I hear you Lord. I hear you Lord. I will. I will. Yes I will do it Lord."*

"Do what Mama?"

"Grab hands - all of you, and let's pray."

Mama asked God to heal her daughters from cancer the same way He healed her from cancer when the girls were little. All this time and the sisters never knew about Mama Precious being a cancer survivor. As difficult it was hearing this news, Mama found comfort knowing the same God that delivered and healed her body can do the same for her 4 daughters.

As they ended their prayer with amen, The daughters addressed Mama. Lyna - *"Thank you Mama for telling us."*

Ashley – *"Mama, we love you so much."*

Mercedes – *"Sorry for all the stress I caused you."*

Effie – *"We are one family. No more secrets and no more pain."*

Mama – *"I love all of you. This includes Fatima and Taraji. You kept all my babies' secrets and supported them like friends….no….like sisters are supposed to do. We love you both."*

"Feeling any kind of pain in your body? Tell Somebody - It just might save your life." – Deborah Shirley Pegues

***Body of Cancer - 7 Strong Women
Independently & Collectively !!***

Deborah Shirley Pegues My Life & My Story with Cancer

Having cancer is truly an experience you can't really share because everyone's body is different – everyone's cancer is different. The stages are different meaning you can be stage 1-2-3-4. It is difficult to talk about. I watched m mother and sisters go through it, and I never thought it would hit me. I kept hurting in my lower part of my body. I went to the doctor, and they kept giving me all kinds of medication – just guessing with my life. Then I went to the GYN Department; thinking since I am a female, they might could help me. They did a biopsy on me, and something came back positive, but they said it was nothing a little cream could cure. I used the cream for about a month – the problem was still there. I decided to make an appointment to be seen in the Gastroenterology Department. My baby sister Raynell encouraged me to go there because they had helped her.

I had an upper gastrointestinal and a GI Endoscopy. This is a test that allows your doctor o look at the inside of your esophagus, stomach and the first part of your small intestine (called the duodenum) before any procedure is done. The procedure lasted about 20-30 minutes, and from there I went to recovery room. Completing this test where a tube was placed down my esophagus with a small light at the end of it and…..OMG – They found my problem. All this time I was going to my doctor and Gyn and it took the Gastro Department to locate and identify where the cancer was.

I had the surgery procedure done. Doctors had to remove six inches of my intestines, and they informed me they got it all (the cancer) out. I didn't know whether to cry or shout so I did both. I had been through so much. (This was all 2018). Part of the recovering from this procedure was that I had to have five rods placed in my spine. If I hadn't I was told I would be wheelchair bound. Not wanting that, I completed this surgery. God is good.

I currently have a hernia in my stomach (hiatal hernia) and reflux disease (Gerd) which can be an ulcer or cancer. Some of these conditions are benign and easily treatable, but

I had to go through a lot just to get an answer. Doctors initially wanted to do surgery on the hernia, but they couldn't – why?... The cancer had returned, and this time in my lymph nodes. It is a rare cancer but can be cured. I've been back on chemo for about a year now. There is no timetable, but the doctors say that the chemo is helping towards moving into remission.

I'm now 70 years old. I know tomorrow isn't promised, but I'm not going to sit around and wait for doctors to act like they care. I'm going to tell my story. I love my body, and it's sad to say that there are some doctors that care and some that don't. My doctor only gives me pain medication, but I don't give up. I have had X-rays, GIs, Pet Scans, MRIs – you name it, I've had it.

This is my life. My goal is to obtain my AA Degree in Child Development and to be able to live my life. My mission of The Body of Cancer is I hope that seeing or hearing my story may help someone fighting cancer. Don't ignore the sounds of your body. We only get one, so please take care of it. This is my Story – This is my Life.

ACKNOWLEDGEMENTS

I would like to express my deepest gratitude. First and foremost, I want to thank God and many people who have helped make this book possible. God giving me the strength to keep going when I so wanted to give up. Father God, you are an incredible God.

To My Mother and Grand-Mother.

Mother - As you are watching over me, I still can hear you encouraging me with words like "You can do all things through Christ who strengthens me."

Grandmother – As you are watching over me, I still can hear you encouraging me words like "I raised you to be strong. Now, don't you shed another tear."

To My Family.

My backbone helping me get through this journey. I would need 5-6 books to thank everyone, but here are some names: Jermaine, Tremaine, Tamika, Nick, Josh, Andre, Andrelle, La-La, Sabrina and of course….Kayden.

To My Friends and Colleagues.

Thank you for your invaluable feedback, insight, and encouragement. Your support has been instrumental in shaping my ideas and refining my writing.

The Stage Play Cast of The Body of Cancer: 7 Strong Women.

7 Strong Women: *Robin J. Williams, Nicole Williams, Charlene Richardson, Charlette Richardson, Taylor Smith, Irish Smith, Courtney Banks. Sincere thanks and appreciation.*

Songwriter: *Yvonne C. Cobbs – "I'm Blessed to be Here." Thank you for such an anointed song.*

Director/Videographer: *Kevin Hall Jr. and Earvie Rollins Jr.. Thank you so much for making my vision come to fruition. You contributions and support are appreciated.*

Special Thanks To: *Ashling Cole, Christolenae Thomas, Tamara Edwards, Peace Gospel Choir*

YOU: I want to acknowledge the readers of this book. Your interest and support have been a driving force behind this creation. Getting the word out there concerning the importance of all our health. Understanding how important it is to know recognize warning signs with your own body, and not keeping it to yourself. Knowing that this just might save your life is my sincere hope.

SPONSOR LIST

Aaliyah Smith	Cindy Nailer	Joann Powell	Ray Braxton
Aja Jordan	Clifford Monroe	Joellen Hicks	Raynell Watkins
Alma Ferguson	Connie Berry	Josh Khiev	Robert Lewis Moore Jr.
Andre Moore	Darius Henson	Karen Walton	Robin J. Williams
Andre Russell	Daryl Christian	Keny Harris	Ronell Simmons
Andrelle Russell	Deborah Clayborn	Kevin Owens	Ronnie Smith
Angie Pryor	Dee Johnson	Kevin Owens Jr.	Ruby Pryor
Anzo Dock	Devohn Moore	Krystal McCoy	Sabrina Norsworthy
Arline Clark	Etonya Titus	Lajae D'Shirl Pegues	Sharmaine Taylor
Aubrey Moore	Fabian Gill	Leeosha Nelson	Shawntina Russell
Barbara Cash Cooper	Fannie Fudge	Leilani Hailey	Sokhonn Khiev
Betty Dimmer	Gloria Knockum	Linda Barnett	Sonya Owens
Beverly Gaston	Gloria Moore	Lonnie Khiev	Steven Parker
Beverly Rankins	Gloria Spann Leslie	Marcel Monroe	Susan Adrien
Bobbie Carpenter	Greg Barnett	Margaret Mackney	Tamara Fleming
Carla Dancer	Gwen Johnson	Margie Barnes	Tamika Bennett
Carol Bennett	Helen Granger	Margie Brown	Tamika King
Carol Collins	Helen Moore	Maria Vanegas	Tamika Tyler
Carolyn Pryor	Herman Watkins	Mason Davis	Tanya Monroe
Carolyn Harper	Iris Ellington	Matthew Griffin	Taylor Smith
Carolyn Pryor	Jackie Mungo	Michael Watkins	Tay-Tay McCloud
Chanta Khiev	Jacqueline Scogg	Myesha Harris	Tee-Tee King
Chantan Khiev	James Collins	Myles Davis	Teionna Cunningham
Charlene Richardson	James Jackson	Nick Khiev	Tramaine Hawkins
Charlette Richardson	Jasmine Moore	Nicole Briggs	Treana Bumpers
Chimere Randell	Geraldine Gould	Oneta Dotson	Tremaine Moore
Christolenae Thomas	Jermaine Moore	Pamela McCoy	Vickki Savoy Griffin
Chunsie Collins-Moore	Jessu Watson	Phyllis McLeroy	William Green
Cheryl Dancer	Jewell Davis	Racquel Bobo	Yvonne C. Cobbs

INTRODUCTION

A Message From The Visionary Author

DEBORAH SHIRLEY PEGUES

Poetry Writer, Playwriter, Author of Two Books
(A Mother's Child Taken by Many, The Body of Cancer: 7 Strong Women)

Those who know me, know I am a quiet, easy-going, people person. I love to smile and learn people from their hearts. I am a cheerful giver; a child of God and I love children. I have 3 biological and I adopted 8. I was married to Robert Lewis Moore Sr., who passed away from congestive heart failure.

I believe in knowing your body for yourself. I dedicate this book in the memory of my mother, Marian Barfield, and grandmother, Regurtha Campbell. I wouldn't be who I am today if it weren't for these 2 beautiful women in my life.

Deborah Shirley Pegues

ABOUT THE AUTHOR

Deborah Shirley Pegues is the Founder and Director of Footprint of Many, a non-profit organization for children, youth and families that has been in existence since 1996. Born in Houston, Tx and raised in Oakland, Ca, Deborah is the fifth of six girls. She is a spiritual and motivating individual who is a devoted mother, grandmother, godmother, and foster care parent.

Deborah's continuous love and passion for children is what drives her daily. She enjoys acting, writing plays, poetry, and books. A few of her poems have been published in the Annual American Poetry Book, Collected Whispers International and Who's Who in Poetry. Deborah has had the opportunity to be an extra in movies such as Flubber and CBS television show Midnight Caller.

In Deborah's Words – "It's important for people to know that your body is your temple. Take care of it, you only get one. Knowing that no matter what you go through in life, if you can look up, get up, and don't give up, you're never alone – Faith over Fear."

Deborah's ultimate dream is to see this book become a movie.

INDEX

Printed in the United States
by Baker & Taylor Publisher Services